SO YOU THINK YOU WANT TO START A BUSINESS

7 Simple Steps to Starting Your For-Profit Business

By

Shawn Headley-Williams

Dedication:

This book is dedicated to all the men and women who have braved the idea of starting a business. When starting a business, there will be ups and downs, there will be days you are on top of the world because the momentum is so great, but there will also be days that you want to give up while wondering why you ever got started. I see you, most importantly God sees you and he will give you the desires of your heart if you just keep the faith. To my mom, thank you for showing me what a hard-working woman looks like. To my sisters, your first best friends are your sisters, and thanks for always loving me. To my children Nyekole, Gerrell, and Jordon, you guys have unselfishly shared me with the world for twelve years, I love you for the love and support throughout the years. Jordon, I remember when I had a clothing and coat drive that landed on your 9th birthday and you were so upset because you just wanted to spend time with your mom. After I gave you a couple of dollars and your father took you out, all was right with the world. I will never forget your sacrifice, I love you "baby boy". To my husband and my bonus baby, Kevin and King, boy oh boy you two have entered my life and just settled right into this whirlwind life that I own. I love you two. I am so happy to be your wife and bonus mom, thank you King for always asking me if "I'm done with my meeting" before asking me to make your pizza. Thank you Kevin for being a husband that's not afraid to let me shine, thank you for always being the 1st person to buy my books as they come out, and thank you for pushing me in all of my endeavors and cheering me on along the way. To my step-son Noah, it is my hope one day that you and I will have a loving and lasting bond. We miss you, we love you, and we can't wait to be with you again. My beautiful grandbabies Mila and Khalil, I do this so one day when you have children, you can proudly say, "Your great-grandma was an author". I love you both dearly. To my family in love, thank you for all the love and support, I love you guys! To my best friend Sheniqua, thank you for always pushing me to be great. I thank you for always being by my side in all that I do in this lifetime. I love you always, here's to 30 years of friendship and counting.

Table of Contents

For-Profit -vs- Non-Profit

What's the Difference?

For-profit organization:

A business whose primary goal is making money (a profit), as opposed to a nonprofit organization which usually tends to set goals for earning money to offset the operating costs. Most companies considered to be businesses are for-profit organizations; this includes anything from retail stores to restaurants.

Non-profit organization:

A corporation or an association that conducts business for the benefit of the general public without profit as a motive, however a nonprofit can generate a profitable revenue source.

- While reading this book and going through the various exercises, ask yourself these key questions in your mind while deciding if a nonprofit is right for you.

- Who is in need of your nonprofit organization?

- Will your nonprofit organization bring about real change within the community?

- Are you willing to say "no" to trying to service the whole world?

- Are you ready to choose a mission, expand on it, and perfect it for your community of interest?

- Is there a nonprofit organization out there doing the same thing you would like to do? If so, could a partnership make the efforts greater instead of competing for the same grants?

- Are you willing to put in the time and energy that is required to grow your idea into a successful nonprofit organization?

- How will you align your passion with your cause and turn it into impact for the community?

Introduction

The idea of starting a business sometimes comes from a place of freedom, a place of not wanting to work for anyone, wanting to leave a legacy for your children, and more. For me, it was all the above. I entered the business world starting my very own nonprofit organization, due to the mother in me not wanting to see children have no clothing or coats or haircuts and a new hairstyle for Christmas day. In 2013, I started my daycare with the intention of just doing an after-school program. After your lessons, take a walk with me as I show you how I took this simple idea and turned it into a six-figure business with employees. I've learned along the way that when you have a solid beginning in business, everything else will come along perfectly.

Step 1: Which Corporation is Best for My Business?

Forming your business organization is the single-most-important choice you'll ever make regarding your business. What form your business adopts will affect many factors, many of which will decide the path of your company in the future. Aligning your goals to your business type will be one of the most important steps, so understanding the advantages and disadvantages of each type is very crucial at this step. There are several types of business corporations to choose from. In this step, we will break down each corporation and you will be able to decide with the help of your CPA (if you don't have one now is the time to get one) which corporation is right for you and your business. The different corporation each state offer for your business is as follows:

- Sole Proprietorships

- General Partnership

- Limited Partnership

- Limited Liability Company (LLC)

- Nonprofit Corporation

- S Corporation

- C Corporation

Let's dig deeper about these corporations so you can see the advantages and disadvantages and the tax breaks or not each corporation provides.

Sole Proprietorship:

When electing sole proprietorship for your company this is the simplest and most common form of business ownership. A sole proprietorship is a business owned and run by someone for their own benefit. The business relies on and is dependent on the owner's decisions, so when the owner dies...so does the business.

Advantages:

- All profits go to the owner

- There are very few regulations to follow

- Owners have total flexibility to run the business as they please

- Very few start-up requirements, usually just a business license.

Disadvantages:

- The owner is 100% liable for the business debt

- Ownership of the proprietorship is difficult to transfer

- No distinction between business income and personal income

General Partnership:

When electing to have a general partnership for your business, both owners invest their money and labor and both owners are 100% liable for the business debt. General partnerships also don't require a formal agreement, partnerships can be verbal or even implied.

Advantages:

- Shared resources provide more capital for the business

- Each partner shares the total profits of the business

- Similar flexibility and simple design of a proprietorship

- Formal or informal it is inexpensive to establish the business

Disadvantages:

- Each partner is 100% responsible for debts and losses

- Selling the business faces difficulty due to having to find a new partner

- The partnership ends when any partner decides to end the partnership.

Limited Partnership:

When electing a limited partnership, it has the same advantages and disadvantages as above however you must create a more formal business when electing a Limited partnership. A limited partnership requires you to file a certificate of partnership with the state, and Limited partnerships differ from general because it allows partners to limit their own liability to the business debts according to their portion of ownership or investment within the company.

Corporation:

Corporations are for tax purposes, separate entities and are considered a legal person. This means, among other things, that the profits generated by a corporation are taxed as the "personal income" of the company. Then any income distributed to the shareholders as dividends or profits are taxed again as the personal income of the owner.

Advantages:

- Limits liability of the owner to debts or losses

- Profits and losses belong to the corporation

- Can be transferred to new owners with ease

- Personal assets cannot be seized to pay for business debt

Non-Profit:

A non-profit corporation is similar to a traditional corporation. There's generally a board of directors, as well as donors or financial backers but a non-profit generates no profit, hence the name. A nonprofit is also generated for a cause, generally one that's public, specifically for members of the non-profit, or groups of people.

Step 2: Executive Summary

When creating your business, it is best to have all of your ideas and information well thought out and broken down into several categories. An executive summary, an overview, your target market, mission, and vision statement. With a for-profit business, most businesses have a motto i.e Nike "Just Do It" and you must also recognize what problem did your business see and how does your business plan on solving the problem. For example, I want to make shea butter because in the winter people's skin gets so dry (problem), when individuals put on my shea butter my product will add moisture to their skin and hold the moisture all day (solution).

During this activity, you will create your executive summary for your business, don't forget your key inputs when creating your summary.

_____

_____

_____

_____

_____

_____

_____

_____

_____

_____

_____

_____

_____

_____

_____

_____

_____

_____

_____

_____

_____

_____

_____

_____

_____

_____

_____

_____

_____

_____

_____

_____

_____

_____

_____

_____

_____

_____

_____

_____

_____

_____

_____

Step 3: Overview

When creating an overview, you must add key points to your overview. In this exercise, you will create your overview with the key points of your business i.e, your history, management team, location, mission statement, and your legal structure. Below begin to create your business overview.

During this activity, you will create your overview with the key points mention to create a solid overview.

_____

_____

_____

_____

_____

_____

_____

_____

_____

_____

_____

_____

_____

_____

_____

_____

_____

_____

_____

_____

_____

Nike's Mission Statement:

"To bring inspiration and innovation to every athlete in the world if you have a body, you are an athlete."

Nike's Motto:

"Just Do It!"

Step 4: Mission & Vision Statements Matter

It is very important to learn the meaning of a mission statement and the difference between mission and vision. Once you have recognized the path of your business, your business will need a mission statement that it will get recognized for. What is a mission and vision statement? A mission statement defines the company's business, objectives, and approach to reach those objectives. A vision statement describes the desired future position of the company. Elements of mission and vision statements are often combined to provide a statement of the company's purposes, goals, and values.

When creating your mission statement keep in mind your mission statement should be a powerful statement that will represent your business followed by a powerful vision statement. Also, keep in mind as you see throughout the book, your mission statement must stand out to the point that as you build your business your mission statement will "speak for" you. Your mission statement will be able to be read and an individual or company will recognize your organization simply by reading your mission statement.

During this next exercise, let's create a mission statement. I have provided you with some keywords that most businesses adopt to put inside of their mission statement to gain power through just words.

Keywords that make your mission statement stand out:

Accomplish	Mediate
Brighten	Facilitate
Create	Practice
Command	Lead
Dream	Knows
Educate	customer
Embrace	Improve

Explore	Live
Give	Inspire
Manifest	Identify

Using 25-30 words, create your business mission statements. Throughout the book, you will see examples of mission statements of businesses that we've used or may have seen. Your mission statement should be short and impactful and easy to remember, just in case you must do an elevator pitch or a 60-second overview of your business.

_____

_____

_____

_____

_____

_____

_____

_____

_____

_____

_____

_____

_____

_____

_____

_____

_____

_____

_____

_____

_____

_____

_____

_____

_____

_____

_____

_____

_____

_____

_____

_____

_____

_____

_____

_____

_____

_____

Now that you have an idea of what your mission statement is going to say, now you must create a vision statement. Keep in mind your vision statement is also a very short yet powerful statement. Most vision statements are simple and are usually one line.

During this exercise, create your vision statement with the space provided.

_____

_____

_____

_____

_____

_____

_____

_____

_____

_____

_____

_____

_____

_____

_____

_____

_____

_____

Essentia Overachieving H2o Mission Statement:

"Keeping you hydrated so you can do the things that matter most to you."

Step 5: Who is my target market?

Most people that get into business forget to research their potential target market. I've heard so many people who start a business and say, I have a large family, so I'll have support... WRONG! You don't go into business to sell your products or service to your family. Although it's great to get support from your loved ones, it really shouldn't be expected. Finding your target market will allow you to understand who your customer is and will allow you to go after who your product or service speaks to.

In this next exercise begin to do your research, let's look up who your target market is and begin to jot down ideas of who will benefit from your product or service and why.

_____

_____

_____

_____

_____

_____

_____

_____

_____

_____

_____

_____

_____

_____

_____

_____

_____

_____

_____

_____

_____

Step 6: Be Ready, So You Don't Have To Get Ready!

I remember going to a networking event, there was a young lady who mentioned she had attended an event but didn't know how to ask for what she wanted. An investor came up to her and as they began to chat, he became very interested in her business. He asked how he could help her with her business and she couldn't answer him. She wasn't ready for someone willing and able to help her. She missed her opportunity to have someone invest in her business. Don't let this scenario happen to you! Be ready, so you don't ever have to get ready!

In this next exercise you will rehearse your "elevator pitch", so when you're asking an investor or a grant-maker for funding you will be able to articulate what your business is all about. Be sure you can explain:

- What your business is about?

- Why does someone need your product?

- How can they partner with you to push your business forward?

Remember that your elevator pitch/30-second pitch is not supposed to be long and drawn out. Your pitch is supposed to be short but filled with important information about you and your business's plans. If the investor is interested, they will make an appointment with you to have a more formal sit-down about your business.

In this activity, you will create a 30-second elevator pitch. A 30-second elevator pitch is important to have. Imagine yourself at a function with investors, imagine an investor coming to you telling you he has a million dollars to give away, but you only have 30 seconds to tell him your business idea; what do you do? You create a 30-second elevator pitch. If you can't come up with a 30-second elevator pitch, memorize your mission statement! The goals of your for-profit business are within the mission and vision statements and will explain your plan on how to make your mission happen.

_____

_____

_____

Step 7: What need is my business addressing and what problem will it solve?

When starting a business most of the time we don't realize we are solving a problem. For example, individuals like myself who start skincare lines usually are aiming for individuals that are interested in ways to have better skin and hydrated skin. In this last exercise, you are going to think about what your business will do for your customers? Is there a need for your products? Are you helping individuals with that need if so, how?

Congratulations You Just Wrote Your First Business Plan!

Congratulation, you've just written the answers to questions in a basic business plan. You can take what you've learned and now transfer all of your responses and create a business plan, you never have to ask anyone to write your business plan again, the questions you've answered in this book are the questions addressed in a business plan.

Now that you've read the book and went through the steps of creating your for-profit business, you should have decided if starting a for-profit is for you. Whether you start your paperwork with a coach or take the brave steps to start your paperwork on your own, I hope that reading this book has made your new beginning a little easier.

Wait! There's more, read how I started my daycare and how I raised it to be a six-figure business. Learn from me how I took the idea of starting an after-school program to running a daycare to six-figures with employees.

Welcome to the World of Business

I started Happy Hearts Day Care in 2013 with the intention of supplementing my income. After dealing with so many landlords in apartments that were just slum lords, I decided to go into whole-house rentals. In 2013 I was just tired of everything. Tired of my job, tired of slum lords, just tired. I rented a house in Long Island, New York. It was time to start to build my business, my kids and I handed out flyers and began to promote the daycare. I applied to be a vendor for the Department of Social Services (DSS) and got to work. By 2014 I was up and running and by 2015, DSS was my favorite three letters. DSS helps working families pay for their childcare and they would pay a small fee. I like DSS because I knew the average person couldn't afford real daycare prices. This was one of my biggest mistakes, not charging what I was worth. It wasn't my business if they couldn't pay real childcare prices or if they couldn't afford DSS, I should've just charged my price and not worry about the rest.

I wanted my daycare to be different, I wanted to stand out from the rest. I opened at 6 am and closed at 7 pm. I soon realized that was a big mistake because parents still came in late. Yes, with a 7 pm closing I still had latecomers. That summer as we pressed on, I created a five-borough tour where I took the kids on a trip in all five boroughs including pool time. There were days that the parents were waiting for their children because I was committed to showing their children a great time.

I knew I had a great program, so I ended the summer with reconstruction, I gave the daycare a new face, I created a daycare policy and late fees in writing, and had parents signed the daycare policy. I started to take my business more seriously and started setting boundaries. I started to hold my parents accountable for their lateness and started to close at 6 pm like the rest of the daycares in the neighborhood. The one thing that stayed the same, I treated the kids like they were mine for the twelve hours they were in my care. At Christmas time, my nonprofit gave each kid toys and various donations. I had a cousin who also donated to my nonprofit for the kids to have an amazing Christmas.

I had a good heart, I got all the perks of running the daycare to cover my business, down to a food allowance. I would feed my children breakfast, lunch, snacks, and dinner. I didn't feed them dinner like normal daycare's which is something to hold them over until they ate dinner at home, in most cases what I fed was the dinner. I was on a high, my parents loved me, the children loved me. My daughter and I ran the business, we were close to our parents, Happy Hearts Day Care was one big Happy Family...or was it? I thought I was close to my parents while most parents were grateful for my service, others were only pretending to be close to take advantage of my kindness.

I've dedicated my life to children, so taking care of children was the job that I've created for myself in one year was nothing surprising.

I began to see in that year that one of my families in my daycare was having some family issues. One of my baby's mom started calling me on the weekend because he used to tell her he wanted Ms. Shawn. I had just recovered from a blood clot on my lungs so going out was not on the table, so I began to take him during the weekend for a couple of hours. Never, cross a boundary with a client. This was one of my biggest mistakes in business, I didn't set boundaries with my parents and I soon would we regret it.

My relationships with my parents came to the point where they no longer feared if they didn't pay their weekly fee, they would come to pick up their child and go home and tell me they would pay me next week. This became such a problem, some of my employees would be upset because they couldn't get their full pay. This brought me so much anxiety and sadness because I don't like to make it my business not to do right by people. My DSS checks were amazing, that's when they came. DSS checks would be erratic to the point I couldn't even depend on that to pay my staff. This combination of getting too comfortable with my parents and my parents not paying consistently was another mistake that I made and want anyone within the sound of my voice to know, not creating boundaries in your business, is a BIG no, no.

Five years in, I had a daycare family have their children stay in my home because they had no lights, had the children some time come on the weekend and the mom asked me to be their children's godmother, which I would soon find out, she only did that to manipulate the situation even more. Why didn't I say no? Why didn't I draw the line in the sand? I'll tell you why, I was too scared to lose the success I had gained and that is no way to control your business. You draw clear lines in the sand and you ask for the pay you are worth. It was to the point these families would come to pick up their children late.

One day on a Friday, I call the father to come get his children due to me not being able to find their mother. The father began to curse me out and told me he wasn't going to pick up his children and told me that I needed to find their mother. After being cursed out, I threatened to bring the children to the precinct; two hours after daycare was over the dad came to get the children. Monday morning, I told the mom and dad that the children weren't allowed back until the late fees were paid, the father eventually paid the late fee. My son was upset about the events, so he told my daycare parent to watch how he talk to his mother. The parent proceeded to swing, and all hell broke loose inside of the daycare. The children had to be taken downstairs to the basement while the parent was forcefully escorted out of the daycare. The father left the daycare and called his wife to tell her that we jumped him inside the daycare. Do you think after this I let the family go? NOPE, I still feared that the success that I had gained would be affected, so I simply banned the father from the daycare when I should of let that family go. I kept the family until the father felt a way and the mom took the kids out of the daycare with owing a fee. I sent in a fee owed letter to DSS so that she couldn't go and do this to another daycare. My daycare lasted for seven years with all of the ups and downs and trials and tribulations. I've seen six-figures and have seen so many great families come through our doors. I have also experienced families that took advantage of the boundaries that I didn't set into place.

Life had it that I started to lose parents for things like family issues, cursing out their worker at DSS and the worker kicking them off the program, and more. I started to see how God was moving me in a direction of letting something go that was meant to only be there to transition me out of school safety. I couldn't let go, I tried everything even took a daycare photoshoot with some of the children to try and revive my image. I was holding on for dear life. I created this, I built this from earning the bare minimum to six-figures with staff, where did I go wrong? I had been wanting to break free from the daycare for so long but was bound in fear. In 2020, the pandemic hit and forced closure for the health safety of the children. During the pandemic, I got married; now was as good of a time as any to get the fresh start I craved. I sent out a message to the parents that Happy Hearts Day Care after seven years will be closing its doors for good, my heart hurt, it was like letting go of a child that you watch grow from a baby to an adult.

I still own and operate Each One Teach One Mentoring service, and I currently charge my clients what I am worth because I give out a wealth of knowledge and I treat this business not as a hobby but as a job.

As I teach each client how to start their business, the biggest thing I want them to take away from me starting and closing a business is, charge what you are worth and create boundaries because you will always have a client that wants to get a discount and you will always have a client who will make you feel a way because they are using your service. Do you know what I say? All money isn't good money and the client isn't always right especially when they are trying to get over on you.

Do you need a coach?

Here's how to contact me:

Should you feel the need to go through the process of starting your for-profit or non-profit business with a coach, you can contact me, and I will gladly help you through your vision.

Shawn Headley-Williams, Executive Director of Each One Teach One Mentoring Service

Email: nonprofitmentor2@gmail.com

Phone: 516-547-0207

Connect with me on social media

Facebook: Each One Teach One Mentoring Service

Instagram: eachone_teach1

What are the clients saying!

Client Testimonial:

After memorizing her mission statement and perfecting her elevator pitch approach one client was able to get a partnership that will provide in-kind grants for her organization.

D. French writes:

This company wants to partner with me, I did my elevator pitch "Thank God"! It was major, they want to sponsor a lot (i.e. computers, training, and help with fundraising)!

A. Jennings writes:

I am grateful for Shawn Headley, founder of Each One Teach One Mentoring Service. She helped me establish two successful businesses "Leaders of the Future No Limits" (nonprofit) and "A.M.E Media Inc.". Her nonprofit class was awesome, yesterday I was asked by someone from the Mayor's office what's your mission and I was able to proudly say! He was so impressed with our mission, In the back of my mind, I was like, thanks Shawn.

S. Garcia writes:

Shawn is amazing, I just want to say thanks for everything!

L. Tillmon writes:

Very informative! I worked for different not-for-profit agencies for years and learned many things that were simplified by Ms. Shawn, the instructor. She is knowledgeable of the ins and outs to get your business started!

J. Cross writes:

The course today was amazing. Not only was it informative but the knowledge shared amongst the ladies and me was life-changing. You will definitely leave this course educated and motivated to get the ball rolling on new innovative ways to use expand your nonprofit.

B. McLean writes:

I took the course and loved it! I met great people and gained so much knowledge.

J. Wilson write:

Today was EPIC!!! This woman is the truth. She provided the tools, clarity, & resources. No questions were unanswered. I would recommend her 100 xs, it's a pleasure doing business with her. She is a non-profit guru.

N. Repass writes:

On Saturday, May 14th I went to an amazing class given by Ms. Headley. The information was awesome, the knowledge she has is amazing. I'm so glad she will be helping me with my nonprofit.

Books by Shawn Headley-Williams

- The Start Is What Stops Most People: 7 Simple Steps To Starting Your Non-Profit Organization

- The Start Is What Stops Most People: 7 Simple Steps To Starting Your Non-Profit Organization—MINISTRY EDITION

- King's Chronicles: A Day In The Life Of Autism

Notes

_____
_____
_____
_____
_____
_____
_____
_____
_____
_____
_____
_____
_____
_____
_____
_____
_____
_____
_____

Notes

_____

_____

_____

_____

_____

_____

_____

_____

_____

_____

_____

_____

_____

_____

_____

_____

_____

_____

_____

_____